LOVE BITES
Caricatures by James Gillray

Todd Porterfield

ASHMOLEAN

LOVE BITES Caricatures by James Gillray
Ashmolean Museum, University of Oxford
26 March–21 June 2015

©Ashmolean Museum, University of Oxford, 2015

British Library Cataloguing-in-Publication Data

A catalogue record for this book is available from the British Library

EAN 13: 978-1-85444-298-7

Design and layout by Baseline Arts, Oxford
Typeset in Foundry Sans
Printed by Windrush Press, Oxfordshire

For further details of Ashmolean titles please visit:
www.ashmolean.org/shop

We are most grateful to the Warden and Scholars of New College Oxford for lending all the works in the exhibition.

Supported by Bridgeman Images

The exhibition was generously supported by the Paul Mellon Centre for Studies in British Art and the Friends of the Ashmolean.

The exhibition has been made possible by the provision of insurance through the Government Indemnity Scheme. The Ashmolean Museum would like to thank HM Government for providing Government Indemnity and the Department for Culture, Media and Sport and Arts Council England for arranging the indemnity.

The author would like to thank Ersy Contogouris and his Gillray seminar students at the Université de Montréal, as well as Benoît Bolduc, Michael Burden and the Fellows of New College. And also to all the staff at the Ashmolean Museum who have helped to bring the exhibition to life.

He dedicates this work, with gratitude, to his family in France, les Khaïat.

Cover image:
*ENCHANTMENTS lately seen upon the Mountains of WALES,
— or — Shon-ap-Morgan's Reconcilement to the Fairy Princess*
30 June 1796
Etching, hand-coloured

Introduction

Born in 1756, a contemporary of Canova, David, and Goya, as well as William Blake, James Gillray was amongst caricature's first full-time practitioners, celebrated for his incisive ridiculing of royal and parliamentary politics and for his unerring anti-French-Revolutionary propaganda. In exile on Saint Helena, Napoleon is said to have bitterly declared that the engraver did more than all the armies of Europe to bring him down. In 1806 the Weimar journal, *London und Paris*, proclaimed him "one of Europe's greatest artists".

On the two hundredth anniversary of Gillray's death, *Love Bites* proposes a selection from the unparalleled collection of New College, Oxford, which holds examples of more than two-thirds of Gillray's 1000-plus prints. We invite visitors to savour and question a selection that treats not separation and hierarchy but fusion and embrace, not hatred and division, but love, sex, and friendship, characters and forms that join, comingle, absorb, bite, slap, marry, cavort, and caress. Our interests are thematic and formal.

If our theme seems familiar, it is not because it is timeless and universal. On the contrary: it is because Gillray and his generation drew battle lines over love, sex, and the family that may still be recognisable today. Against the tumult of social unrest, conservatives such as Edmund Burke pretended that marriage and the patriarchal family provided an unchanging norm, a bedrock foundation for monarchical authority and the nation. For radicals like Mary Wollstonecraft, love and friendship — autonomous undertakings of equals with no sanction by the state — were the germ of political virtue that would lead to a progressive public realm, while her partner (and, secretly, her husband), William Godwin (1756–1836) declared that "marriage was an institution that held couples hostage to their transient passions".

As for Gillray, in his personal life, he never married, though writers have speculated that he might have been romantically involved with his friend and publisher, the equally never-married and only in name "Mrs" Hannah Humphreys. For a long time the artist lived above the shop, and Humphreys cared for him to the end of his life when he was insane and suicidal. In one of the few accounts of his life, the celebrity fencing instructor Henry Angelo reported that Gillray and Humphreys, ready to marry, made it as far as the church of Saint James, before turning back, deciding at the last minute that it really wasn't necessary at all.

On a formal and art historical level, Gillray's engravings and later lithographs emerged into a nascent mass culture, seeming to broadcast at lightning speed to a limitless public, yet their bulging forms and bulbous lines draw from august traditions of high art. In his dotage, Gillray greeted George Cruikshank, who had come to pay his respects. "My name is not Gillray", said the old man, "but Rubens". Gillray collected engravings after Rubens, and we might see in his works an updating of Rubens's variety, fecundity, ripeness and embrace, one of the more enchanting aspects of his art. We might also consider him in the broader history of art, a wide-eyed and acerbic addition to a canon of artists of love that includes Rubens, Boucher, and Brancusi.

Oppositions

To set our subject in relief, let us begin not with love but with hostile conflict.

In the 18th century, caricature flourished in a rapidly expanding press. It stoked parliamentary factionalism and modern nationalism. In its bid to reveal essential identities, it posited that each individual and nation had a fixed character that was legible based on appearance and manner. Caricature thereby contributed to the development of the modern stereotype.

☉ *PHAETON Alarm'd!*
22 March 1808
Etching, engraving and aquatint, hand-coloured

PHAETON alarm'd! _

Now all the horrors of the heavns he spies,
And monstrous shadows of prodigious size,
That, deckd with stars, he redtens oer the skies.

T' astonishd youth, where eir his eye could turn
Beheld the universe around him burn:
The world was in a blaze!

In this first section, Gillray employs old-fashioned allegory, adapts portraiture and deploys the pseudo-science of physiognomy.

PHAETON Alarm'd! *(previous page)*

Gillray casts Foreign Minister George Canning in the role of Phaeton, the son of Apollo, who disastrously attempted to drive his father's chariot across the sky. Dignified by his classical nudity, and pulled by his cabinet ministers, Canning must face a nightmarish array of hybrid monsters, portraits of his political opponents. On the burning earth below, Napoleon rides the Russian bear.

HANGING. [Fatal Effects of the French Defeat.] DROWNING.

Prime Minister Pitt, and War Minister Dundas (right) and Opposition leader Fox (left) respond to news of Allied

↻ *HANGING. [Fatal Effects of the French Defeat.] DROWNING.*
9 November 1795
Etching, hand-coloured (printed, *c.*1830)

victories over the French. In the tradition of the religious diptych, the line between the two images joins and also separates political opponents. It can hardly be said to create a moral contrast, as it brings together the desperately suicidal with sloppy, drunken degeneracy.

French Liberty/British Slavery

Writing in 1874, French critic and Gillray enthusiast, Champfleury contrasted meagre French Revolutionary caricatures with British ones, which are violent and extreme, and "make one think of a slice of bloody roastbeef". It is this particular side of England, in art as in cooking, which shows itself to be red, fat, nourishing, and apoplectic.

Do we not cut a pale figure compared to our neighbours whose blood is injected with fattening food, stimulating drinks, and purgatives that require stomachs of bronze?

↻ *French Liberty/British Slavery*
Published 12 December 1792
Etching, hand-coloured

FRENCH LIBERTY.   BRITISH SLAVERY.

DOUBLÛRES of Characters; — or — striking Resemblances in Phisiognomy. — "If you would know Mens Hearts, look in their Faces".

I. The Patron of Liberty — Doublûre. The Arch-Fiend. | II. A Friend to his Country — Doubt. Judas selling his Master. | III. Character of High Birth. — Doubt. Silenus debauching. | IV. A Faithful Patriot. — Doubt. The lowest Spirit of Hell. | V. Arbiter Elegantiarum. — Doubt. Sixteen-string Jack. | VI. Strong Sense. — Doubt. A Baboon. | VII. A Pillar of the State — Doubt. A Newmarket Jockey.

DOUBLÛRES of Characters; — or — striking Resemblances in Phisiognomy. — "If you would know Mens Hearts, look in their Faces".

Celebrity fencing master and memoirist Henry Angelo said that informed beholders consider this "the *ne plus ultra* of caricature".

Gillray's depictions of Whig leaders portray their essential characters as devils, squanderers, drunks, gamblers and baboons. Using Lavater's theory that physiognomy reveals inner character, the artist succeeded, according to a Tory Lord who thanked him: "The opposition are as low as we can wish them. You have been of infinite service in lowering them and making them ridiculous".

Might we ask, though, why Gillray needs a second portrait and extra attributes for each man? Might there be some even inadvertent admission that identity, like appearance, is not singular and permanent but shifting, composite and contingent?

⌒ *DOUBLÛRES of Characters; — or — striking Resemblances in Phisiognomy. — "If you would know Mens Hearts, look in their Faces"*
1 November 1798
Etching, hand-coloured

"Two Pair of Portraits"; presented to all the unbiased electors of Great Britain, by John Horne Tooke.

In the 1788 pamphlet *Two Pair of Portraits*, John Horne Tooke used the conceit of a portrait catalogue, criticising Fox and in praise of Pitt. Ten years later Gillray skewers Tooke for changing sides.

Gillray thus delivers a parodox of caricature. Fox's incompetence and Pitt's benevolence are consistent in their fathers' portraits behind the easel, but the portrait painter is a liar and a turncoat.

☼ *"Two Pair of Portraits"; presented to all the unbiased electors of Great Britain, by John Horne Tooke*
1 December 1798
Etching, hand-coloured

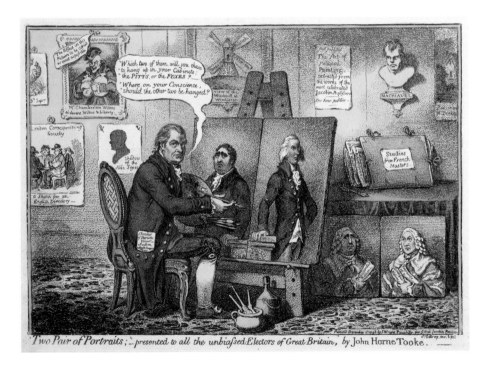

Assimilation

How can a group, or even an individual, have an identity and coherence when it is inevitably made of disparate parts?

This section features prints that explore the modern quandary of how to make a whole when faced with otherness, when that which is outside appears suspiciously unmalleable to our interests, when recalcitrant material may not become what we want it to become.

Design for the NAVAL PILLAR

Gillray's *Design* came out during an abortive competition for a naval monument.

War trophies of an imagined victory over the French — a flag, a cannon, a Revolutionary bonnet, and even sailors' legs and backsides peppered with gunshot — bulge but conform to the colossal sculpture's cylindrical form. Triumphant Britannia rules the seas.

⊙ *Design for the NAVAL PILLAR*
1 February 1800
Etching and aquatint, hand-coloured

"The Trident is confirm'd:____ *Adapted from The Pursuits of Literature; in Dia. 4th & the Note.*

Design for the NAVAL PILLAR.

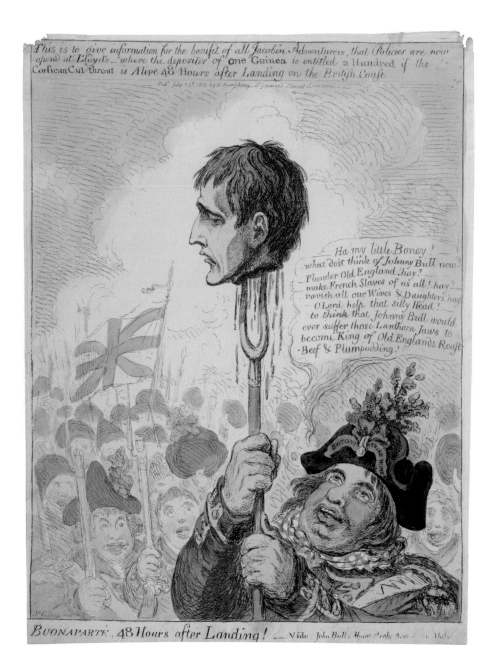

BUONAPARTE, 48 Hours after Landing! — Vide. John Bull. Home Strok &c.

Buonaparte: 48 Hours after Landing!

Deflecting fear of French invasion, Gillray imagines victory. The pink and round-faced crowd jeers. The portrait of Bonaparte, 'the Corsican Cut-throat', recalls an antique coin and prints of the guillotined in France — pale, linear, seen in profile, and dripping with blood. With this trophy at the end of John Bull's pitchfork, French Revolutionary head-cutting is assimilated to British art and British fantasies of revenge.

G *Buonaparte: 48 Hours after Landing!*
26 July 1803
Etching, hand-coloured

MIDAS, Transmuting all into ~~GOLD~~ PAPER

A French landing in Wales led to a bank run in late February 1797, the suspension of the pound's backing by gold reserves, and to the printing of the first one and two pound paper notes. Gillray quickly responded.

Stationed at a chamber pot, like a Midas in reverse, Pitt has assimilated the nation's gold reserves to his heaving stomach, but he emits mostly paper. His opponents, carping nearby in the reeds, reject the equation of gold and paper. In Gillray's title, "Gold" has been crossed out but stands next to and is not subsumed into "Paper."

⟳ *MIDAS, Transmuting all into ~~GOLD~~ PAPER*
9 March 1797
Etching, hand-coloured

MIDAS, Transmuting all into **GOLD** *PAPER.*

History of Midas,— The great Midas having dedicated himself to Bacchus, obtained from that Deity the Power of changing all he Touched; Apollo fixed Asses Ears upon his head, for his Ignorance — & although he tried to hide his disgrace, with a Regal Cap, yet the very Sedges which grew from the Mud of the Pactolus, whispered out his Infamy, whenever they were agitated by the Wind from the opposite Shore.— Vide Ovids Metamorph.

Merging

Alternatives to binary oppositions include Gillray's forms and characters that merge, achieving total unity, symbiosis or penetration. Each entity might or might not maintain its distinct character. This promiscuity of form and content disturbed Gillray's detractors who reigned from the 19th to mid-20th centuries, when Gillray's reputation was at its low ebb.

In Maurice and Cooper's 1904 history of caricature, Gillray's pictures come from an unclean and unbalanced mind and evince "physical deformity" that "symbolises the moral foulness of the age". They show "bloated faces; twisted, swollen limbs, unshapely figures whose protuberant flesh suggests a tumefied and fungoid growth - such is the brood begotten by Gillray's pencil, like the malignant spawn of some forgotten circle of the lower inferno".

An Excrescence; – a Fungus; – alias – a Toadstool upon a Dung-hill.

The fungal roots of Pitt's chinless profile curve into the form of a crown, nourished by muck, driven by ambition.

In December 1788, a handbill blasted 'Prince Pitt' for his 'undue exertion of the Prerogatives of the Crown', for raising himself above it and 'seizing on the Sovereignty of these Kingdoms'.

↻ *An Excrescence; – a Fungus; – alias –
a Toadstool upon a Dung-hill.*
20 December 1791
Etching with engraving, modern hand-
colouring

ENCHANTMENTS lately seen upon the Mountains of WALES, ___ or ___ Shon-ap-Morgan's Reconcilement to the Fairy Princess.

ENCHANTMENTS lately seen upon the Mountains of WALES, — or — Shon-ap-Morgan's Reconcilement to the Fairy Princess

Enchantments marks the long-awaited reconciliation between the notoriously randy Prince of Wales and Princess Caroline.

Set against a primitive landscape, supporters dance a folksy round and the king appears out of the sky to blast detractors from their perch. The befeathered princess and the reluctant goat differ in gesture, girth, gaze, colour and texture. Yet together they coalesce in a pleasingly voluptuous form.

⌃ *ENCHANTMENTS lately seen upon the Mountains of WALES, — or — Shon-ap-Morgan's Reconcilement to the Fairy Princess*
30 June 1796
Etching, hand-coloured

Fashionable Contrasts; – or – The Duchess's little shoe yielding to the magnitude of the Duke's foot
(not exhibited)

In late 1791, the Duke of York married Frederica of Prussia, known for her exquisitely tiny feet. In one of art history's most eloquent examples of fragmentation and abbreviation, which deliciously evoke a scene that happens mostly outside the pictorial field, Gillray celebrates their merging.

↺ *Fashionable Contrasts; – or – The Duchess's little shoe yielding to the magnitude of the Duke's foot*
24 January 1792
Etching, hand-coloured
© The Trustees of the British Museum

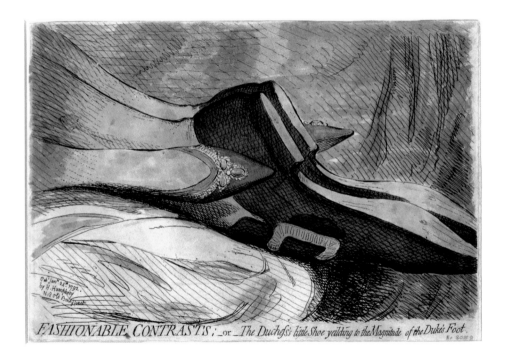

FASHIONABLE CONTRASTS; _ or _ The Duchess's little Shoe yielding to the Magnitude of the Duke's Foot.

LUBBER'S-HOLE, – alias – The Crack'd JORDAN

Gillray imagines the Duke of Clarence, more or less still dressed in his naval gear, diving into a Jordan or chamber pot. The image is a play on the name of his mistress, the celebrated actress Dorothy Jordan, his lover for twenty years.

Excluded from the two-volume 1851 Gillray catalogue, it and *Wha Wants Me?* were reprinted in the optional extra volume of 45 so-called suppressed plates for those of less delicate sensibilities.

↪ *LUBBER'S-HOLE, – alias – The Crack'd JORDAN*
1 November 1791
Etching, hand-coloured

LUBBER'S-HOLE,_alias_The Crack'd JORDAN.

Couples

Pairs, partners, companions and couples are found throughout Gillray's work, their inspiration drawn from antiquity, art history, mathematics, aesthetic challenges, celebrity, politics and contemporary street life. They are never uninformed by questions of class, race, gender and the body.

Foremost among them are images of friendship. In political theory in England, on the Continent and in the United States, friendship was a model for disinterested amity, as distinguished from family ties. Marriage was a different matter again.

A Sphere, projecting against a Plane

Gillray well understood that a humourist had to be above all a brilliant thinker of form and that sex and geometry were intimately tied. The principle at first mystified our contemporary, the philosopher Slavoj Žizekž, when he heard a joke that began: "What happens when a triangle meets a circle"? "How could that be funny if it does not hurt?" he protested. But then he realised, "What if I was wrong, what if I missed the purely formal aspect that is what makes a joke much more funny than its direct content, in the same way that sexuality is not a matter of direct content, but of the way this content is formally treated".

In *A Sphere, projecting against a Plane*, the pained and diffident Pitt and the lascivious and spheroid Countess of Buckinghamshire barely touch at a single point. This Gillray explained in the theorem placed below the title:

Definitions from Euclid. Def: Ist B: 4th. A Sphere is a Figure bounded by a Convex surface; it is the most perfect of all forms; its Properties are generated from its Centre; and it possesses a larger Area than any other Figure.—Def: 2d B: Ist A Plane, is a perfectly even & regular Surface, it is the most

A SPHERE, projecting against a PLANE.

Definitions from Euclid. Def:1st. B:4th. A Sphere, is a Figure bounded by a Convex surface; it is the most perfect of all forms; its Properties are generated from its Centre; and it possesses a larger Area than any other Figure.— Def:2d. B:1st. A PLANE, is a perfectly even & regular Surface; it is the most Simple of all Figures; it has neither the Properties of Length or of Breadth; and when applied ever so closely to a SPHERE, can only touch its Superficies, without being able to enter it — Vide. Euclid, illustrated, by the Honble. Mrs. Circumference.

Simple of all Figures; it has neither the Properties of Length or of Breadth; and when applied ever so closely to a Sphere, can only touch its superficies, without being able to enter it—

⌂ *A Sphere, projecting against a Plane*
3 January 1792
Etching, hand-coloured

The Twin Stars, *CASTOR & POLLUX*.

The Twin Stars: Castor and Pollux

The May 1789 series, *The New Pantheon of Democratic Mythology*, parodied members of parliament, including George Barclay and Charles Sturt from Dorset, here presented as the legendary twins from antiquity, Castor and Pollux. When the demigod Castor died, his mortal twin Pollux asked to share his immortality, so the two were transformed into stars, the constellation, Gemini.

In ancient statuary, Castor and Pollux lift their hands to rein in horses. Here they hold aloft beers. They seem like a rather jolly pair, happy and buoyant, despite their considerable girth. Improbably rising, they are like inflated putti imported from Rubens, now mature and ripe.

G *The Twin Stars: Castor and Pollux*
7 May 1799
Etching, hand-coloured

Pylades and Orestes

From antiquity to the present, the Greek cousins Pylades and Orestes have been, in Ovid's words, "a true model of love". In the Renaissance they embodied the eternal character and value of friendship, and in the 18th century the purity of their devotion stood apart from political corruption. Unlike other male pairs in antiquity, who were typically complementary types, they were nearly identical, according to Victor Hugo, as close as O and P in the alphabet. For Lavater, reproducing Benjamin West's 1766 portrayals, they were "the embodiment of the harmony between physical and moral beauty".

Resonating with this tradition, Gillray offered a clear-eyed, humble and realistic model of the best that human ties can offer. In the guise of Pylades and Orestes but comically distinguishable and prosaic, the Prince of Orange and his secretary Nasselin are seen, as they often were, shuffling along Bond Street. Nasselin would support the prince, who was narcoleptic, and so tripping and falling asleep. Rather than representing spiritual and physical perfection and heroic sacrifice, they walk stupidly, but gamely, into the void.

→ *Pylades and Orestes*
1 April 1797
Etching, hand-coloured

J.^sG.^y ad vivum fec.^t

Kisses Private and Political

A recurring image in Western art from Rubens to Rodin, the kiss is the opposite of Oppositions. It joins. It accepts and bridges difference. It unites through artistic compositions and narratives, across politics and nationalities, and in personal and amorous relations. Sentimentalists might see private kisses as timeless and universal, but Gillray's are neither, not in an age, like all ages, when amorous and political affiliations are contested, even policed. Perhaps they are the quintessential caricature subject because, like the fraudulent but effective kiss of Judas, they can betray.

The Blessings of Peace, The Curses of War

During a period of war-induced rural food shortages, the Crown and Anchor Society commissioned this exceedingly conventional engraving to stoke fear of a French invasion.

On the left, The Blessings of Peace is a thoroughgoing rustic genre scene of domestic, marital, and patriarchal bliss. It is centred on the hearth and home, the table complete with characteristically English roast beef. The tidy cottage is reminiscent of Gainsborough's rural idylls, as if the industrial revolution had never come to England, and the child's kiss binds the family. On the right, however, The Curses of War threaten death, destruction, and the murder of the father.

⤴ *The Blessings of Peace, The Curses of War*
12 January 1795
Etching

Such *BRITAIN* was! — Such *FLANDERS*, *SPAIN*, *HOLLAND*, now is!

from such a sad reverse
O GRACIOUS GOD,
preserve Our
Country !!

Design'd & Engrav'd
by I.ᵗ G.ᵗ
for the Chairman & Members
of the Crown & Anchor Society.

Pub.ᵈ Jan.ʳ 12ᵗʰ 1795, by H.Humphrey N.ᵒ 18 New Bond Street.

The Blessings of
PEACE,
PROSPERITY & DOMESTICK-HAPPINESS.

The Curses of
WAR,
INVASION, MASSACRE & DESOLATION.

To the PEOPLE & the PARLIAMENT of Great-Britain, this Print is dedicated.
by the Crown & Anchor Society.

"Curs'd be the Man who owes his Greatness to his Country's Ruin !!!!!

The first Kiss this Ten Years! — or — the meeting of Britannia & Citizen François

In 1795 the philosopher Kant had declared that we must have peace because the world is round. To seal the deal on an 1802 peace treaty, Bonaparte and Britannia kiss, forming a spherical whole.

Despite Citizen François's declaration of 'everlasting attachment', the Peace of Amiens lasted only until May 1803.

G The first Kiss this Ten Years! — or — the meeting of Britannia & Citizen François
1 January 1803
Etching and aquatint, hand-coloured

Murder! – murder! Rape! – murder!
O you Villain! – what have I kept my Honor
untainted so long, to have it broke up, by you at last? –
O Murder! – Rape! – Ravishment! – Ruin! Ruin! – Ruin!!!
BANK of ENGLAND
LOANS
J.G. d. & fec.
POLITICAL-RAVISHMENT, – or – The Old Lady of Threadneedle-Street in danger!
Pub May 22d 1797. by H Humphrey St James's Street

POLITICAL-RAVISHMENT, — or — The Old Lady of Threadneedle-Street in danger!

A French landing in Wales led to a bank run in late February 1797 and the suspension of the pound's backing by gold reserves (which lasted until 1821), spurring Gillray's inaugural presentation of the Bank of England as the Old Lady of Threadneedle Street.

War-time Prime Minister Pitt's "rape" of the bank targets the dwindling gold reserve and ignores the newly issued one and two-pound notes. Political instability and unceasing propaganda in England and France contributed to the untrustworthiness of printed matter — an ironic avowal by a maker of prints on paper, whose apprenticeship included designs for banknotes.

POLITICAL-RAVISHMENT, — or — The Old Lady of Threadneedle-Street in danger!
22 May 1797
Etching, hand-coloured

The RECONCILIATION

The reconciliation of George III and the Prince of Wales is played out as the Biblical parable of the prodigal son who returns to the arms of his father, a time-honoured pictorial subject.

The dissolute appearance of Gillray's prince scandalised English and German newspapers. However, the protagonists are locked in a moving embrace. On a surprisingly equal footing, their upper bodies bridge the chasm, the prince's head in his father's bosom.

↻ *The RECONCILIATION*
20 November 1804
Etching, hand-coloured after 1800

The RECONCILIATION. [And he arose and came to his Father, and his Father saw him, & had compassion & ran, & fell on his Neck, & kissed him. Read the Parable. Verse 16th to 24th]

CUPID

The half-blind MP John Nicholls gracelessly aims his arrow at his next target. The image was one of Gillray's *New Pantheon of Democratic Mythology* series, which satirises Whig politicians in the guise of Greek mythological figures.

—— ci-devant Occupations :—or—— Madame Talian and the Empress Josephine dancing Naked before Barrass in the Winter of 1797—— A Fact!——

Barrass (then in Power) being tired of Josephine, promised Buonaparte, a promotion, on condition that he would take her off his hands:—Barrass had, as usual, drank freely & placed Buonaparte behind a Screen, while he amused himself with these two Ladies, who were then his humble dependents.—Madame Talian is a beautiful Woman, tall & elegant: Josephine is smaller & thin, with bad Teeth something like Cloves.—it is needless to add that Buonaparte accepted the Promotion & the Lady.—— Empress of France!

⤷ —ci-devant Occupations—or—
Madame Talian and the Empress
Josephine dancing Naked before Barrass
in the Winter of 1797—A Fact!—
20 February 1805
Etching and aquatint, printed after 1848

—ci-devant Occupations—or—Madame Talian and the Empress Josephine dancing Naked before Barrass in the Winter of 1797—A Fact!—

The drunken and enthroned Barras, leader of the post-Revolutionary Directoire, squints, while Bonaparte ogles Barras's naked lovers, Josephine and Madame Tallien through a gauzy muslin. Rumour had it that Barras had tired of Josephine and palmed her off on Bonaparte as part of the deal in which the young general became commander in chief of the Army of Italy. This is how careers and men were made.

⟳ CUPID
7 May 1799
Etching, hand-coloured

The INTRODUCTION

The Duke of York introduces his new bride to his parents.
The miserly king and queen jump out of their thrones with
excitement at the sight of the money the young woman
brings to the marriage.

⤵ *The INTRODUCTION*
22 November 1791
Etching, hand-coloured after 1800

Marriage

Gillray's marriage pictures intervene in debates about matrimony.

In 18th-century common law, marriage makes two become one — easier said than done. In playing on clichés of classical timelessness, of marital harmony, and of nature's bounty, our artist shows that such platitudes can do nothing to guarantee union and harmony.

While new laws imposed religious and bureaucratic requirements on most people, and obliged the King's children to seek parental permission to marry, some political theorists found marriage a prison, especially for women.

◐ *The Marriage of Cupid and Psyche*
3 May 1797
Etching, printed c.1830

Gillray reveals and plays on society's fear of partnerships that are undertaken in freedom and equality.

The Marriage of Cupid and Psyche *(previous page)*

The wedding of the Earl of Derby and the great actress Elizabeth Farren is reproduced in the guise of the first-century antique cameo, *The Marlborough Gem*. Celebrated for centuries, the original cameo was once owned by Rubens. The classical pedigree of the image heightens our sense of the mismatch of the flabby and nearly immobile groom and the emaciated and towering bride. The flame having gone out, there is little hope that reproduction will follow.

The Morning after Marriage-- or--A scene on the Continent

In 1785, the Prince of Wales and Mrs Fitzherbert, (who was Catholic and twice-divorced), married secretly and illegally without the king's permission. In 1788, Gillray shows the honeymoon. The prince, like the candle, is spent, while she beckons for more.

Gillray's prince echoes the posture and degeneracy of both husband and wife in Hogarth's moralising *Marriage à la Mode*. In Gillray, illegitimacy abounds, but we are refreshingly spared moral lessons.

↪ *The Morning after Marriage-- or--A scene on the Continent*
5 April 1788
Hand-coloured etching and engraving

The MORNING after MARRIAGE __ or __ A scene on the Continent

Democratic levelling; - Alliance a la françoise;__or__ the Union of the Coronet & Clyster-pipe

Fox joins in matrimony Lady Stanhope and her family's apothecary, who is constructed out of medical equipment. Politicians Stanhope and Sheridan, dressed as French revolutionary *sans-culottes*, attend.

An anti-democratic or 'anti-leveller' club probably commissioned this, one of Gillray's most iconic compositions, which recalls and upends the piety of Raphael's *Marriage of the Virgin*.

The unholy ceremony takes place beneath the guillotine, that 'Shrine of Equality,' evoking the terror caused by such class-crossing alliances. Here are the monstrous and destructive results of a society of freedom and equality.

⮫ *Democratic levelling; - Alliance a la françoise;__or__ the Union of the Coronet & Clyster-pipe*
4 March 1796
Hand-coloured etching

SHRINE of EQUALITY.

Rights of Man

Democratic Leveling;___ Alliance a la Françoise;___ or ___ The Union of the Coronet & Clyster-pipe.

Lord Stanhope.   Lady L. R. Stanhope.   Fox.   Homer Taylor   Sheridan.

Three in a Dynastic Bed

Threesomes involving the Prince of Wales are featured in this section. Gillray may criticise the prince (for his rudeness, for instance) but he does not take a moral standpoint toward trios, which he depicts as sometimes harmonious and sometimes fraught.

BANDELURES

Mrs Fitzherbert is seated between a blithe Prince of Wales, who plays with a *bandelure* (a yoyo, symbol of frivolity) and Sheridan, who was staying temporarily at Mrs Fitzherbert's with his wife. Sheridan leers and gropes, giving a creepy tinge to what is otherwise a rollicking threesome. With the soft touch of the etcher's needle, they voluptuously merge on a comfortably padded couch, brought together by cascading, rounded forms.

➲ *BANDELURES*
28 February 1791
Etching

BANDELURES.

t!
n secure,
Man
true;

London Pub'd Feb: 18. 1791. by S.W. Fores, N.º 3, Piccadilly.
Mr Fitzherbert

P. Wales

Fond Fool, arouse! shake off thy childish Dream,
Behold Love's falshood, Friendships perjur'd troth;
Nor sit & sleep, for all around the World,
Thy shame is known, while thou alone art blind—

Sheridan

Blachmore—

Gilroy

FASHIONABLE-JOCKEYSHIP

A bony Lord Jersey carries the obese Prince of Wales to
Lady Jersey's bed — not only acquiescing to, but generously
facilitating his wife's affair with the prince.

🎧 *FASHIONABLE-JOCKEYSHIP*
June 1 1796
Hand-coloured etching

Bites, Swallows, Strikes

Rather than kisses that unite, here we have meetings of opponents through swallowing, poking, spanking, ingesting, and biting, and so we are close to the etcher-caricaturist's own practice. Cruel, elegant, painful, vulgar, and absurd, they might teach lessons, hold at bay, or destroy.

Power struggles are revealed, dissimulated, and trumpeted in physical — and sometimes prosthetic — contact carried out in a spirit of play, elegant grace, and upending hostility, in which civilisations, nations, political parties, men and women, and their diseased and healthy bodies are at war. In ritual ingestion or cannibalisation, a new age might be born.

☉ *The Vulture of the Constitution*
3 January 1789
Etching and aquatint

The VULTURE of the CONSTITUTION.

The Vulture of the Constitution *(previous page)*

During the king's bout of insanity, Pitt and the Prince of Wales fought for power. As on an emblem or coin, Pitt is as elegant as a vulture could be, clamping talons on the prince's crown, ingesting the other bird's feathers.

The scene plays out on a distant peak, against indistinguishable space achieved through light velvety effects of aquatint. Deep space evokes deep time and the epochal stakes for monarchical rule.

The Republican rattle-snake fascinating the Bedford-squirrel

Fox is the snake in the garden about to capture the Duke of Bedford, who recently acted to limit their opponent Burke's pension. Earlier in his career, Gillray associated the snake with the American Revolution. Caricaturists will pick up on the visual trope of vermin falling into the mouth of a revolutionary during the French Commune.

↪ *The Republican rattle-snake fascinating the Bedford-squirrel*
16 November 1795
Etching, hand-coloured

The Republican Rattle-Snake fascinating the Bedford-Squirrel.

Pub.ᵈ Nov.ᵗ 16ᵗʰ 1795. by
H.Humphrey New Bond S.ᵗ

The Rattle Snake is a Creature of the greatest subtilty;—when it is desirous of preying upon any Animal which is in a
situation above itself, it fixes its Eye upon the unsuspecting object, & by the noise of its Rattle fascinates & confounds the unfortunate
Victim, till loosing all Sense & discernment, it falls a prey into the Mouth of the horrid Monster. Plinÿs Nat. Hist.ʸ ʸ vol 345.—

"*L'Insurrection de l'Institut Amphibie*." _____ The Pursuit of Knowledge.

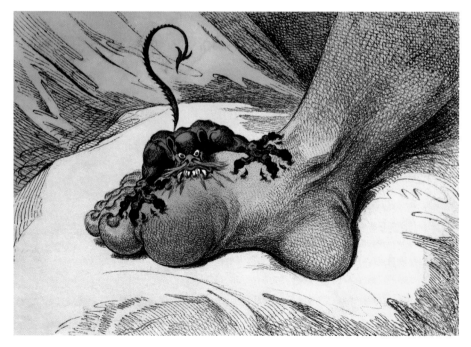

"L'Insurrection de l'Institut Amphibie". ___The Pursuit of Knowledge.

France invaded and then occupied Egypt in 1798 to challenge England's presence in the 'Orient'. Under the guise of spreading civilisation, Europe's modern colonial era had begun. Bonaparte established the research-oriented Institut d'Egypte, but Gillray and the crocodile tell us what they think of Universal Enlightenment.

The artist adds another note of modern doubt by facetiously insisting on 'Impartiality and Fidelity', as if this were copied from an 'original, intercepted drawing'.

The GOUT

How could an etcher of Gillray's ways not aspire to the effect of gout, which attacked bloated, wealthy men of the 18th century. In 1861 *Blackwood's* Magazine explained its effect:

> *"the demon Gout sticks his fangs into your toe, and thenceforward claims you as his property. Woe to the individual upon whom gout once sets his mark, for there is no kind of fumigation or exorcism powerful enough to drive him away... There is a grim sportiveness about gout, which reminds us forcibly of the manner in which a tomcat plays with a mouse. After a severe clawing, a respite of some duration is allowed to the victim...vain delusion!!"*

G *"L'Insurrection de l'Institut Amphibie". ___The Pursuit of Knowledge.*
12 March 1799
Etching, hand-coloured

G *The GOUT*
14 May 1799
Soft ground etching with engraving and roulette, hand-coloured

The Collector's Caress

In the hothouse economy of love and art, the relationship of the amateur (from the Latin amator, or lover) to an object often takes the form of intense desire. The collector wants an object, pursues, handles, and possesses it in a process and with a vocabulary not dissimilar to courtship. While the collector can be subsumed in his or her passion for an object, the desired object is not human and remains 'other,' ultimately unattainable, yet with the potential to threaten the balance of power between gazer and gazed, owner and owned.

A Peep at Christies; — or — Tally-ho, & his Nimeney-pimmeney taking the Morning Lounge

The Earl of Derby and his mistress Elizabeth Farren gaze attentively at paintings that express their hidden desires. Derby was awaiting the death of his terminally ill wife so that he could marry Farren. The sensual atmosphere of the caricature is underlined by the representation of Susannah and the Elders, observed by the three figures in the background.

⮌ *A Peep at Christies; — or — Tally-ho, & his Nimeney-pimmeney taking the Morning Lounge*
24 September 1796
Etching and aquatint, hand-coloured

A Peep at Christies ;—or—Tally-ho, & his Nimeney-pimmeney taking the Morning Lounge.

A COGNOCENTI contemplating y͏ͤ Beauties of y͏ͤ Antique.

A COGNOCENTI, contemplating ye Beauties of ye Antique

The collector Sir William Hamilton examines a classical bust of his young wife Emma. Even seen through backwards glasses, she is a beautiful object for his collection — a true trophy wife. Emma Hamilton, however, retains some autonomy as she gazes back. Behind her on the wall we see her in a portrait as Cleopatra grouped with her lover Nelson as Mark Antony and a landscape of an erupting volcano.

◔ *A COGNOCENTI, contemplating ye*
Beauties of ye Antique
11 February 1801
Hand-coloured etching

CONNOISSEURS examining a Collection of GEORGE MORLAND'S

Gillray mocks the connoisseurs' earnestness and smug appreciation before popular artist George Morland's lowbrow rural scenes, painted with folksy naturalism. Behind them, the art dealer Mortimer slaps yet another pig portrait up on the wall.

Here is an unvarnished and straight-talking version of love in the barnyard and in the gallery.

⮑ CONNOISSEURS examining a
Collection of GEORGE MORLAND'S
16 November 1807
Etching and aquatint, hand-coloured

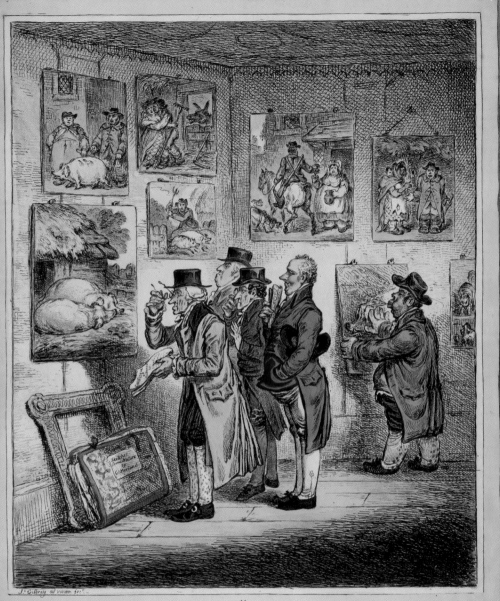

CONNOISSEURS examining a collection of GEORGE MORLAND'S.

London Publish'd Nov.r 16.th 1807. by H Humphrey 27 S.t James's Street.

VERY SLIPPY-WEATHER

Gillray memorably illustrates what will become a cliché of caricature's democratic appeal. A hodgepodge of types from urchin to dandy study a compendium of Gillray's work. The shop is that of his long-time publisher and companion, the never-married 'Mrs' Humphreys. Inside, elite subscribers, including the often-skewered Prince of Wales, retrieve the latest productions.

For their admiration and devotion, Gillray returns the love, serving up a man falling on his rear.

G *VERY SLIPPY-WEATHER*
10 February 1808
Etching, hand-coloured

Conclusion

JAMES GILLRAY'S MANIFESTO ON LOVE

From this experience of Gillray's prints, we might deduce *Gillray's Manifesto on Love and Caricature*, which might go something like this.

Our looking at Gillray is historically inflected. We have no pure, immediate, and eternally true access to Gillray and his intentions. In his day English politicians recognised and feared his effectiveness. Napoleon saluted him for his anti-French influence, and the Weimar journal *London und Paris* declared him one of Europe's greatest artists. His reputation fell into ignominy in the Victorian era, particularly the more sexually tinged pictures, ten of which from our exhibition, were held back from the 1851 Gillray catalogue, and featured only in a by-request-only volume of "The Suppressed Plates". Gillray's notoriety lasted until after World War II, and a recent outpouring of Gillray studies was sparked by the 2001 Tate exhibition, in which Richard Godfrey quipped that Gillray practiced "caricature without a conscience". A man for our day.

Love, like artistic reputations, friendships, and affiliations is not timeless and universal, but contingent and politically informed.

The singularity and coherent identity of individuals and nations is neither stable, true, nor fixed. Identity is always plural, no matter how much art history-- and Leonardo's Vitruvian man-- would attempt to say otherwise. Otherness is always within.

In caricature, illegitimacy abounds. It is not only a theme but, with the most belligerently truthful caricaturists, it is also a posture, an admission of the practices' own incapacities to guarantee legitimacy and its own unwillingness to try.

In caricature, the long-standing distinction between social and political caricature does not hold.

In caricature, form matters. Gillray's choices of artistic precedents-- be it Raphael or Rubens-- show it. Our artist's favoured elaboration of curves, globes, and coalescing flesh harken back to Rubens, who is updated and desacralised for the modern age.

The upshot is that there is no guarantee of legitimacy, neither in art, nor in social status, nor in declarations of belonging. Deprived of these assurances, a space is opened up for the leeway and judgment of the spectator, who can decide on these alliances for him or herself, though he may fall on his ass.

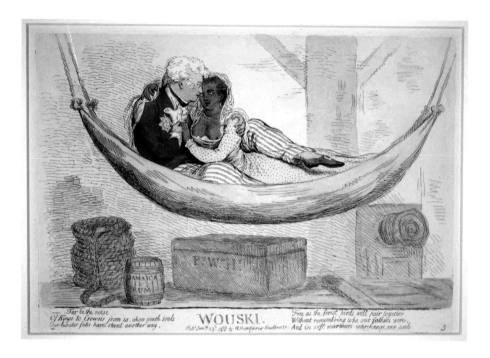

Far be the noise
Of Kings & Crowns from us, whose gentle souls
Our harder fate have steel'd another way.

WOUSKI.

Pub.d Jan.y 23.d 1788 by H.Humphrey New Bond St.

Free as the forest birds well pair together
Without remembring who our fathers were,
And in soft murmurs interchange our souls.

Wouski *(not exhibited)*

In the wake of a popular comic opera by George Colman the Younger, which featured "Wouwski," a black servant, and with rumours swirling around that Prince William, Duke of Clarence had purchased a Creole woman in Jamaica and brought her back to England, Gillray's *Wouski* is formally simple, thematically impassive, and even brutally elegant. The gentle curve of the hammock cradles the lovers and locks in place the composition beneath the ship's deck, suspended between a barrel of rum, product of the vast Jamaican slave labour, and the ship's cannon, by which Britain rules the seas. In the face of abundant evidence of imperial violence that would give rise to such a coupling, Gillray's prince sings a blithe song of utter freedom, "Free as the forest birds we'll pair together/Without remembering who our fathers were."

Wouski
23 Januray 1788
Etching, hand-coloured
© The Trustees of the British Museum